# IF WISHES WERE HORSES
# THE POOR WOULD RIDE

*poems by*

## Clare Louise Harmon

*Finishing Line Press*
Georgetown, Kentucky

# If Wishes Were Horses
# The Poor Would Ride

## ACKNOWLEDGMENTS

YOUR NAME IT IS LIKE THE LIGHT and THE BUBBLE first appeared in
*Tammy Journal* #5

IF WISHES WERE HORSES THE POOR WOULD RIDE (I-II), THE
SARTORIALIST, LADIES, GENTLEMEN, FLUID-PILE ENCHIRIDION,
SUSPENSION THEORY, and FEAR OF INCLEMENT WEATHER (I-V) first
appeared in *The Stockholm Review of Literature* #6

Editor: Christen Kincaid

Cover Art: Clare Louise Harmon

Author Photo: Clare Louise Harmon

Cover Design: Clare Louise Harmon

Printed in the USA on acid-free paper.
Order online: www.finishinglinepress.com
            also available on amazon.com

Author inquiries and mail orders:
Finishing Line Press
P. O. Box 1626
Georgetown, Kentucky 40324
U. S. A.

# Table of Contents

*For Ken, Tom, Sarah, Yuri, David, and Isoa.*
*Gratitudes always, despite what the text may seem to say.*

# IF WISHES WERE HORSES THE POOR WOULD RIDE (I)

[Redacted] began playing violin at age 10          comparatively late
to the company she would keep          later in life.
The daughter of a poet/postal accountant
and a trained          though not practicing          actress
[Redacted] felt          from a tender age
an obligation to succeed          as a musician          at all costs.
Although talented and bright          she would spend   her entire life
attempting to compensate   for lost time          and inadequate
technical facility   or          "chops" in musician parlance.
[Redacted] auditioned for music school at age 16
after only a year          of private lessons.
Not surprisingly          she was summarily          and swiftly          rejected.
After a preliminary audition          at Northwestern University [Redacted]
an esteemed pedagogue and Bienen School professor          went so far
as to call [Redacted]'s parents          to a meeting
to shame them          for squandering   their daughter's potential
saying something   like:

*If only          you had sent her          to me          when she   was three*
*she could have been          a great          soloist.*
*But now   she'll have to quit          anything else          would be          a waste.*
*But don't worry          she seems smart          maybe          she could be a doctor.*

# IF WISHES WERE HORSES THE POOR WOULD RIDE (II)

In a timely        though not uncommon switch
for failed violinists        such as herself
[Redacted] began playing the viola at age 17    under the tutelage
of [Redacted]    a graduate of the Juilliard School    and Yale University.
Once described as a "walking exclamation mark"        [Redacted]
supervised        what he termed    "Viola Bootcamp."
[Redacted] was to learn        the totality of etudes    by D.C. Dounis
a notorious and controversial figure  in string pedagogy.
Wishing nothing other than to overcome    childhood deficiencies
[Redacted] dutifully practiced    the carpal-busting etudes responsible
according to numerous anecdotes    for more than one
career-ending    injury.


On lesson days        [Redacted] allotted
an extra thirty minutes    to her travel time.
within which to excise        in a gas station
bathroom        on the corner of 56th and France
the anxiety        that manifested as nausea
and culminated    in vomit.
The ritual concluded with a purchase        of gum
tic-tacs        altoids  or the like        an attending necessity
for her arrival at the lesson    moments later
flush-faced        mint-tinged        depleted and faint.

# "YOUR NAME IT IS LIKE THE LIGHT"

*Votre âme est un paysage choisi*
*Que vont charmant masques et bergamasques*
*Jouant du luth et dansant et quasi*
*Tristes sous leurs déguisements fantasques.*

[Redacted] was born in Uzbekistan
sometime mid-century           1952       or possibly earlier.
He studied with members of the [Redacted] Quartet       and later taught
at the [Redacted] Conservatoire       and the [Redacted] Academy in Tel Aviv.
He married his sonata partner       [Redacted]       and asks her to play
with those students       who cannot afford to pay       a pianist.
On Tuesday mornings       at approximately 10am       he requests
that his 9am lesson       fetch for him the skim milk latte
(two packets of Splenda).
When he opens his mouth to voice this desire       his studio colors
in cigars tartar       and Listerine       (though really       maybe simply
some woodland creature       in black  putrefaction).
He often drives his students       to doctor's appointments
once       an oral surgery       more than once
the emergency room       the train station
and a rock and roll concert  in Detroit.
He routinely sweats   through several shirts       in a single day       of teaching.
As a result       his wife [Redacted]       packs
neatly folded button-ups       instead       of lunches.
He believes women are not suited       to be performers
but       likes the bodies       in the outfits       always looking       so nice.
[Redacted] speaks English   with Italian grammar
and once asked       if Debussy       was my namesake.

3

# THE EDWARDIAN SITUATION (I)

[Redacted] was orphaned at age 8.
His parents tragically expired        when the family business
a restaurant        bar        and nightclub        burned to bric-a-brac        ash-pile.
[Redacted] survived        with little.
Where he went for care and shelter   immediately following
this disaster        is unknown.
In the subsequent years        [Redacted] expressed near-savant ability
in both music        and mathematics   but as is often the case
with prodigious promise        [Redacted]'s gifts   were scattered.
He lacked the discipline for either field        and as a violist
his chosen instrument
his technique        seriously        lagged.
When [Redacted] auditioned for university study        he was accepted
on straightforward        if restrictive terms.
He would play no chamber music        sonatas   or new music.
He would be confined        to the back        of the viola section
quarantined        like an eighteenth-century leper.
He would live        in a Tudor-style mansion   with his teacher   and her husband
where his eight-hour practice sessions
would be        methodically        monitored.
The agreement was simple  actually
[Redacted] would devote
his late-adolescence        to study  in exchange        for a future
as a performer and pedagogue        a carefully crafted        duplicate
fully broken        able        and poised.

# THE EDWARDIAN SITUATION (II)


Prior to her three-year appointment  with the [Redacted] Symphony Orchestra
[Redacted] spent time                    in Toronto.
You see  despite a successful audition          for the violin studio
at [Redacted] University    not to mention              her unquestioned
virtuosity        [Redacted]        was not permitted to matriculate
due to insufficient scores   on the TOEFL exam.
Due to her storied talent   a compromise    was reached.
[Redacted] would live in Toronto with her intended teacher
and re-apply      for academic study        the following year.
The agreement was simple  actually
help      with a few household chores    in exchange
for room and board         ESL courses
and a politically    and musically invaluable    mentorship.
Months into the arrangement        original promises
remained unfulfilled        [Redacted]
received  no linguistic instruction      and her lessons   were few and far between.
Though          in point of fact            this was  for much the better
as [Redacted] had little          time or energy to practice    following grueling
fourteen-hour days        of innumerable    domestic            tasks
including thrice daily        meal preparation  from shopping to clean-up.
The Edwardian situation    escalated slow    yet consistent      over time.
[Redacted] was eventually    forbidden    to call home      or leave the house
save a weekly      accompanied reprieve                to grocery shop.
It was during one of these outings    that [Redacted] escaped    her servitude
turned down      an aisle  baking      paper products      canned vegetables
fled              leaving behind              her violin
and assorted      though not specified      personal mementos.

# THE SARTORIALIST

For a recent performance    of Tchaikovsky's *Souvenir de Florence*
[Redacted] donned        a white  silk      tunic.
Even under the glow       of minimal stage lighting
the garment       took on an explosive sheen.
It forced his chamber music partners  into temporary blindness   and had also
the unpleasant consequence        of disorienting audience members
unfortunate enough       to sit    in the front row.

Years prior       when [Redacted] arrived in the States
to study with [Redacted]    or rather          "[Redacted]"
at the Manhattan School    he sat    with the same manner       of bravado
at the back       of the New York Philharmonic      viola section.
In response       the regular subs he supplanted             posed
with somewhat diluted      vitriol
*Who the hell is this kid       taking my gig?*

[Redacted] would later       establish himself   as a charismatic hotshot
principal violist     of Tonhalle in Zurich       sought after soloist
chamber musician and clinician.
Though more generally      [Redacted] is known as an ego
with big hands     and a small
viola.

# THE BUBBLE
*(for I.C.)*

[Redacted]       teaches       approximately   sixty     hour-long
violin lessons per week       and practices until 1am    nearly every day.

*Manifestations vary but may include the following symptoms*

Many of his advanced pupils      go on to attend
prestigious east-coast institutions    of higher learning
and when queried about their success     he most usually remarks
"We worked hard.      I hope she/he does well there."

*Abdominal organ sacs swell and inevitably burst: dough in a pressure-packed spiral*

Not yet indoctrinated     to American     Neo-Victorian frigidity
one of his five-year-old students    wrote him a note of gratitude
that simply read       "I love you"
when what she meant      was "thank you."

*Gilded sclera forms fatted crust fastened upon the eye or lipidonous golden gristle addendum*

At 41       [Redacted] has few     personal possessions
a painting      authored by a family friend
a framed and autographed poster   commemorating
the Detroit release      of J Dilla's 2003 album   *Ruff Draft.*

*Bones crumble dusty grit like dog-eared pages of first-edition Foucault—finger-twixt*

Books are scarce  though some choice volumes     remain
pedagogical treatises     highlights     of post-structural thought
and a single volume     that rests     honorific
upon [Redacted]'s bedside table   and holds within   the inscription
"My Dearest [Redacted]:   To read this   is to know  that you are not alone."

*Neurological brain scatters distress in fits starts seizure or speech and strut staggered*

It is suspected                        that [Redacted]        suffers from Gaucher's Disease
though he does his very best            to keep secret                    his illness.
When concerned friends     gently confront     [Redacted]
about his health    and or sizable      often debilitating   medical bills
he evades deftly    with either a witticism        or intrapersonal freeze.

*Depending on onset and severity patients may live to adulthood*

[Redacted] attempts to maintain friendships    with colleagues he finds "cool"
that is to say        sincere                and curious
and once noted    with puckish poignancy     that life              would be better
would that we lived in a bubble        together            safe     from all things.

# LADIES

Ginette Neveu died in a plane crash  only a few years after winning
the Henryk Wieniawski International Violin Competition.
With her in the fated cabin          her brother and sonata partner
the boxer Marcel Cerdan    rumored to be              Edith Piaf's lover
and forty eight others        dearly            departed.
Her entire discography      is available        on a set of four    LPs
that includes the Brahms and Sibelius violin concerti
lyrical miniatures  by Fritz Kreisler and Josef Suk
Debussy's            violin sonata              and the *Tzigane*
a virtuosic showpiece            by Maurice Ravel.
Among collectors and connoisseurs  this remaining document
of Neveu's playing is prized          and considered            unparalleled.
Often     these same          discriminating audiophiles describe  her as a great
"lady-virtuoso"    distinguished
from her contemporaries   Oistrakh  Szeryng            and Goldberg
by her warmth              unbridled passion  and capability to embrace
her public with a supple      sonic      touch.
According to lore transmitted                from witness      to press
to public        when her body was found
among the wreckage        she was still clutching
her Stradivarius    holding it          "like an infant."

# GENTLEMEN

Szymon Goldberg        served as concertmaster
of the Berlin Philharmonic between the years 1929        and 1934
under Wilhelm Furtwängler        an iconic interpreter        of Beethoven.
Prior to this appointment   he spent several years in Dresden
at the behest of his teacher Carl Flesch.
According to popular legend        and        more formal oral histories   passed
from teacher        to student        and back again
it was through the heroism of the violist        Paul Hindemith
a close friend        and chamber music partner
that Goldberg escaped        Nazi warcrimes.
However        this has yet to be verified    by any reliable source.
From 1942        to 1945        Goldberg was detained in Java
where he was considered    a prisoner        of war.
This three-year internment  appears in his obituary
as nothing more    than a footnote.
His Brahms sonatas        recorded with Arthur Balsam
evince        the desperation    into which he so gracefully tapped.
That is to say        the space round the notes    like        the field round the body
is sacred active        ether    or        ever-stalking        nothing
the that which comes prior  and or        is left behind.
To the present day        his disciples speak still        of "Mr. Goldberg"
and lament wistful        their once limited        now expired
contact   with the great violinist        pedagogue        and person.

# WORKING GIRL

[Redacted] coolly approached
the podium
*I thought*      *you might like*      *to see these*
she said
as she placed
precariously adjacent
to an Urtext score
of Mahler 4      marked to perfection
her iPhone      lit      unlocked      vulnerable      even.
The conductor tapped and swiped      grimaced      in rosed face
as he read      the left-justified      "from" column
authored by his male colleague      the then-present concertmaster.
The acts      addressed to [Redacted]      were deftly described
in digital shorthand      rendered      as follows

*Want 2 fuck u*      *thinking of yr hot wet pussy*      *suck my dick*
*dirty whore*      *put me in yr mouth*    *my head bt yr thighs*      *I'll lick yr cunt*

## FLUID-PILE ENCHIRIDION

"I look at drivers on the freeway as I pass fast in the left;
consider the quantity of waste produced by just one. Just think of it—
the sheer amount of shit and urine and cum by just one."

A native of South Minneapolis                    [Redacted] graduated
from the University of Minnesota     where he was a pupil
of the respected   though personally and professionally
malicious          *[Redacted]*          author   [Redacted].

*Make yourself a wretch and do everything according to rule.*

Throughout this academic career       [Redacted] maintained
markedly defective relationships      with his colleagues          musical
and otherwise                 often thrusting     his detrimental
corporeal preoccupation                 upon friends
and artistic collaborators     alike.

*If the companion is impure he who keeps her company becomes likewise impure.*

More specifically   [Redacted] perniciously pitted person
on person          to tap taught  insecurities     and aggravate
the body-hating culture      oh so very latent
in circles          of western classical performers.

*The body is weak and subject to the restraint and the power of others.*

[Redacted] found his fluid-pile existence          disgusting          and indeed
this self-loathing   culminated in bulimia                  obsessive
practicing          and a pattern of quick shifting        polarity
twixt Stoicism                  and out-and-out   hedonism.

*It is the mark of degeneracy to spend much time on the things which concern the body.*

A voracious reader          [Redacted] applied          his disordered single-
mindedness to consuming   the philosophical canon      in its entirety.
Presumably          his dedication to the ascetic ideal      remains total.

*Your whole soul will be nothing at all if one thing after another pleases you.*

[Redacted]'s          guilt-burden is sizable          and as such          impels him
to destroy          those for whom    he cares most.

*Expect all advantage and harm from yourself.*

At present          he lives with          his wife and son    in East St. Paul
and teaches violin          from his home.

## FEAR OF INCLEMENT WEATHER (I)

[Redacted]       favored horizontal playing.
That is to say       he preferred playing laterally       across all four strings
drawing the bow   forward  and back       through multiple planes
rather than maintaining repeated contact       with a single vertex
while the left hand       shifts up dramatically
toward the nose   and down again.
This of course       or so we can assume   is the legacy of Franco-Belgian technique
specifically that of his teacher   the great composer and virtuoso [Redacted].
Much of twentieth-century viola literature       was written for [Redacted]
and as a result       reflects the aforestated pragmatism   and right hand primacy.
For example       Bela Bartok's Viola Concerto
features extended passages of barriolage
a pattern intended       to be executed     in arpeggiation
wherein the left hand remains  a stable whole   each finger performing easfully
their putted functions   rather than leaping radically     from position to position.
While some students believe  an accurate rendering   of these oft-decried measures
indicates vertical facility       that is to say   elaborate pyrotechnics of the left hand
seasoned veterans former students of [Redacted] and his progeny
recognize it       as a bow-driven exercise
or       a complex       sounding geometry
of the right hand.

## FEAR OF INCLEMENT WEATHER (II)


On December 2nd 1949     Bela Bartok's Viola Concerto
premiered in Minneapolis    under the baton    of [Redacted]
with [Redacted]    the dedicatee      as viola soloist.
In those days        the Minnesota Orchestra     was the Minneapolis Symphony
and performed at Northrop Auditorium
on the campus of the University of Minnesota
as Orchestra Hall          was not yet constructed.
The mid-century Minnesota intelligentsia      likely flocked
to the central mall eager to hear      a great composer's swansong.
And yet  the work despaired        Bartok's intended triumph.
You see  Bartok left the concerto      near completion   in sketches
pending revision   on a rainy day      in September of 1945.
[Redacted]        was to meet with Bartok
at the composer's            upper-Westside apartment
en route          to an engagement in Maine.
They planned to discuss final edits    potential technical difficulties        and or
non-idiomatic              impossibilities
however        the rendezvous never occurred.
[Redacted] forgot his umbrella
and wished to avoid        the inclement weather.
Perhaps he feared        the precipitate would crumple
the perfect crest   of his fedora
streak his overcoat          or perhaps       his viola case
was piped        with suede.
Days later        while [Redacted] performed                something
somewhere        on the Atlantic Coast
Bela Bartok died
leaving the concerto unfinished        raw
and somewhat     unplayable.

## FEAR OF INCLEMENT WEATHER (III)


A kind of bionic man of the viola     [Redacted]
taught at the Curtis Institute    for some fifty years     and continues    even now
to take             new students.
He succeeded his teacher    the great viola virtuoso        [Redacted]
in this position     and disseminates   the Franco-Belgian tradition
to which this mentor        adhered.
[Redacted]'s students rank   among the best violists      in the world
many of them      hold prestigious positions
in the so-called "top five" orchestras.
While his legacy as a pedagogue      is uncontested     unrivaled     monolithic
the realities of [Redacted] as teacher              especially in his later years
include lesson-long naps    on the studio chaise
and a marked disinterest     in his pupils'     public performances.
One such instance occurred with respect to [Redacted]'s student      [Redacted]
now principal violist         of [Redacted].
In the midst of performing  the Bartok Viola Concerto
[Redacted]'s A string snapped            *dry plunk*            *thump*      it went.
Even at the tender age of 21   [Redacted] behaved    as a consummate professional
and thus continued unimpeded       playing the extended passagework
in the highest positions              on the C          G         and D strings.
(that is to say     leaping radically   from position to position)
In the morning after        [Redacted]'s Curtis Institute colleague
and then-concertmaster     of the Philadelphia Orchestra
approached the master-violist
*Heard your student*              *on the radio*
            because you see   in those days     Philadelphia Public Radio
            broadcast all the Curtis Institute     student recitals
*kid sounded great     but were those really  your*        *fingerings?*

# FEAR OF INCLEMENT WEATHER (IV)

[Redacted] won his position          as principal violist
of [Redacted]       in 1994.
Prior to this appointment      [Redacted] spent ten years
as principal of [Redacted]    after attending
the Curtis Institute of Music          in Philadelphia.
Despite these accomplishments      he speaks          humbly  of his past
noting the debt owed to his mentor  [Redacted]
and his mother     a school teacher    amateur cellist
and resident of [Redacted].
His German language skills are formidable  and as such    the conductor [Redacted]
has been known to ask him to translate expressive
markings          in Mahler's symphonic scores.
[Redacted] is tempted      in these situations
to decode the tangled Viennese cipher          into material not fit
for mixed company.
He maintains a small studio          at the University of [Redacted]
where he chain-smokes      before and after    his students' lessons
and has  more than once    been mistaken          for a transient.
He often acts as ringleader for section-wide  practical jokes
designed for good fun      and based      in musical erudition.
His "Titan" prank      is the stuff      of storied legend.
While he is most usually     a sought chamber musician during
the throes of his alcoholism          he lost          a great many gigs
due to an inability      to arrive at rehearsals
sober          on time          or      at all.
[Redacted]'s affable nature    artistic    and personal integrity
made the realities      of his disease      particularly tragic.
There was no doubt  he wished to do right    by his students   colleagues and family
however he was often incapable of doing so   and thus          until he
sought treatment      his cycle of abuse perpetuated
[Redacted] believes    that the western classical musician          is an interpreter
tasked with the faithful representation  of the provided score    and      as such
his playing lacks affectation          deception
and in its dedication      to the musical ideal          it is nearly          Platonic.

## FEAR OF INCLEMENT WEATHER (V)

[Redacted] was given [Redacted]'s
copy      of the Bartok Viola Concerto        clandestinely
on a January afternoon                in 2007              an attempted
dead-drop rendezvous at 1111 Nicollet Avenue
Orchestra Hall              or simply "The Hall."
The pages        some twenty-five years young
were contained in a plastic bag
likely a prophylactic measure                    given the harshness
of Minneapolis winters.
The staples bled rust        onto the signature crease
and the piano part        was long lost.
[Redacted]        was to pass through        the stage door
that is              the entrance      on Marquette Avenue            stop
at the security desk        and ask the gatekeeper
for the package        (*um*      [Redacted] *left*            *a score*    *for me?*)
at precisely        3pm.
She arrived dutifully at 2:55        only to find [Redacted]      chain-smoking
in the granite courtyard adjacent      frigid      score      in plastic bag
in gloved-hand        grinning
broad      if awkward
not knowing quite        how to interact
give this   precious document      cased in crinkling reliquary
inscribed by [Redacted]    bearing ghosted marks of [Redacted]
to his most dedicated      female student              [Redacted].

## SUSPENSION THEORY
*(The Banff Centre Masterclasses)*

Tunnel Mountain is not a mountain
more of a foothill                really
nothing to write home about
but it feels like a movie set  if you've never before topped a peak
quasi-simulated crispness   and every bit of decay                in perfect pile.
Tunnel Mountain has a precipice     not too terribly steep
but enough        to warrant a guard rail              three feet tall and change.
One might climb Tunnel Mountain    or rather hike it
one might do so    to experience nature                etcetera
but really        one climbs it
for the precipice   overlooking the most earth-bound   of the Canadian Rockies.
There      at the precipice               that is
you can see        all manner of resorts       for the rich     pseudo-rustic chalets
you can see even   Lake Louise
pristine waters                like                all the cliches
r.e.        immaculate        mountain vistas   wilderness godheads        etcetera.
You can see it      the glob  gleaming cyan                from the precipice
you can see it                        and when you jump
when you        circumvent the safeties
precautions set by park rangers
you can touch it.
But instead        instead
you call your mother        a nation away      and you say        *I'm sad*
*I'm looking at Lake Louise*    *and I'm going to do it*        *there is no one here*
*I'm going to touch that lake*    *and all it would take to break*    *is me*
*lifting leg*        *over leg*                *body over barrier*
*over arbitrary*                *divide.*


tumble thump                crack crack ricochet        etcetera


I climbed to the top of Tunnel Mountain                and I almost jumped
thought I could    touch that lake                thought I could
and make        martyr                etc.

## GRATITUDES

My deepest thanks to all my workshop colleagues and friends at the University of New Orleans: Tyler Gillespe, Kia Groom, Jessica Morey-Collins, Laurin Jefferson, Joseph Buckley, Spencer Silverthorne, Jessie Strauss, Liz Hogan, Dahlia El-Shafei, Shaina Washington, Lauren Walter, Clare Welsh, Andrew Kindiger, and Maya Lowy.

Love and appreciation to Jennifer Hanks, Jade Hurter, and Jeanne Thornton for listening to these stories and encouraging me to record them in all their horror and humor.

Much and many thanks to Casey Foote for his support, generosity, humor, and kindness.

As ever, I am completely humbled by and grateful for my mentors, Carolyn Hembree, Niyi Osundare, and Justin Maxwell.

**C**lare **Louise Harmon** is a musician and poet. She is the author of *The Thingbody* (Instar Books, 2015) and *If Wishes Were Horses the Poor Would Ride* (Finishing Line Press, 2016). Her work has appeared in numerous magazines and journals including *Sixth Finch, PANK, Tammy, Lockjaw,* and *The Feminist Wire.* An advocate for rape survivors and persons in recovery from eating disorders, she regularly volunteers for The Emily Program as a guest speaker and blogger.

Prior to completing her MFA at the University of New Orleans, Clare trained and worked as a classical musician. After graduate studies at Michigan State University under the tutelage of acclaimed soloist, chamber musician, and conductor Yuri Gandelsman, she taught violin, viola, and chamber music at Drake University and played in the Des Moines Symphony viola section. In 2008 she founded the new music festival Chamber Music Midwest and served as artistic director until 2011. As a performer, she has appeared throughout the US and as a resident artist at the Banff Centre and Le Domaine Forget.

She lives in New Orleans with her rescue chihuahua, Tink.

www.ingramcontent.com/pod-product-compliance
Lightning Source LLC
LaVergne TN
LVHW091236080426
835509LV00009B/1312